The Metamorphosis of Capitalism

Realising Associative Economics

The Metamorphosis of Capitalism

Realising Associative Economics

Christopher Houghton Budd

Associative Economics Institute
Canterbury, England / Neuchâtel, Switzerland

Published 2003
Associative Economics Institute
Canterbury, England / Neuchâtel, Switzerland
www.ae-institute.com

ISBN 0 948229 05 5

A catalogue record for this book is available from
the British Library

Printed by:
Cromwell Press, Trowbridge, England

Disclaimer

Offered in a spirit of on-going research, the publications of the Associative Economics Institute are intended to encourage awareness of associative economics and what this approach can mean for the development of an economic life that is truly in service to humanity. The views expressed in this publication belong nevertheless to their authors.

Gender

In this book, where reference is made to 'one' or to the human being, we have used the masculine. It might be politically correct to use constructions such as h/she, or to alternate gender on a random basis, as some academics now do, but this can look both awkward and ugly. It is also not clear that the charge of masculine domination really holds. It may be that tradition conceals an unspoken meaning, such as when one refers to the soul, or to a ship, for example, as she, rather than it. Moreover, outside of English, the use of gender is integral to many languages, so that the meaning behind its use may not be chauvinism but something quite different and even legitimate. It is perhaps important not to put a wrong emphasis on this matter, therefore. In any event, it is worth mentioning that those who drive change in the modern economic world, whether as consumers, investors or pathfinders, are preponderantly women.

Contents

Foreword

The idea of this book is to show that associative economics not only gives deep historical foundations to our understanding of current events, but also provides positive and practical means to address the many issues these developments give rise to. That said, the associative economic paradigm is not, of course, validated simply by proponents proclaiming its merits. Only future history can be the judge. However, we are that future and the world will be what human beings make of it.

The central theme of this book is the metamorphosis of capitalism, but this does not refer to a political enterprise. However grand a theme in historical terms, it comes down to the challenge we all face to overcome self-centredness in economic life. I believe humanity is well up to such a challenge and that associative economics will unfold to the degree that we have the will to meet what history is now expecting of us.

In this regard, associative economics is both path and instrument. Its thorough-going analysis of the origins and purposes of economic life and its guiding image of a single global economy, characterised by cooperative endeavour and transparent accounting, offer humanity not only an important management tool, but also a means to heighten awareness and undertake transformative action.

A companion volume to *A Human Response to Globalisation*,[1] it begins by setting the stage in 'big picture' terms, then describes the response of associative economics to the challenges facing humanity – first in panoramic, macrosocial terms, then by way of a close-up on an associative way of doing business. The camera then pulls back to look at the possible consequences for future economic life were this approach taken up. The focus goes first to some main implications for conventional economics as generally taught, before returning to the big picture by offering a glimpse at the macroeconomic landscape of monetary policy, financial markets, the role of gold, and related matters.

My aim throughout has been twofold.

---

[1] Marc Desaules, 2003. *A Human Response to Globalisation*. Associative Economics Institute, Canterbury, England and Neuchâtel, Switzerland, 2003.

Firstly, to articulate the main ideas developed over many years of close cooperation with many colleagues, but especially with my Swiss companions, Marc Desaules and Anita Grandjean. Secondly, to sense how such ideas can find their way into the Anglo-Saxon psyche, the 'venue' in my mind for a thorough-going rethink of the nature and purpose of economic life. Having written from a standpoint within that psyche insofar as I represent it. Time will tell whether my assessments in this regard are well-founded.

Christopher Houghton Budd
Canterbury, England
August 2003

1 The Metamorphosis of Capitalism

Alongside progress and cosmopolitanism, today's world also experiences riches amid poverty, increasing insecurity, volatility in finance,[2] and a host of other problems that seriously qualify the 'success story' of modern economic life. There is a serious discrepancy between ideal and outcome, source and estuary. At the source, there is constant iteration of the belief that resources are scarce, that monopoly is bad because collusive and giving rise to high prices, that, therefore, prices need to be kept low, and that competition is the best way to achieve this. At the estuary, extensive over-production, increasing wealth disparities, 'unfaithful' capital, a burgeoning proportion of speculative trade, failing pen-

[2] With finance, we can find ourselves all too easily in an abstract field, in which its meaning can be as elusive as we would like it to be precise! In order not to become snagged on this problem, in this book, 'finance' means the provision and or management of money and capital.

sions, ballooning debt, and entrenching poverty are all signs of serious economic ill health. The hope was for a rising tide on which all boats would float equally; the reality seems to be a race to the bottom, as each one of us tries to beggar the other.

With an anti-globalisation movement becoming larger, more vociferous, and more organised by the day, the situation facing humanity may prove more serious than many believe. A fault line is beginning to develop between those who champion the prevailing orthodoxy and those who critique it – essentially between the advocates of a 'free' economic life and those who see the nation state and the democratic process as providing necessary constraints.

It is not clear, however, whether a 'rapprochement' between these views will be possible. Modern history has seen economic life slip so many regulatory constraints that, even if it should be re-regulated from outside, it is by no means certain that it could be. Whether we are aware of it or not, we are all implicated in the new regime because it works through finance and through competition in finance. We are now wholly accustomed to and dependent upon a world of endless low pricing. To re-constrain economic life – and finance in particular – is to risk out-pricing everything and everybody.

Without some far-reaching change in our understanding of finance and economics, therefore, it is difficult to see how this situation can be reversed. Politically, we may applaud the re-constraining of the economy and of corporations, but economically very few of us would be able to meet the challenges that an end to ever-downward pricing would bring. We may deplore its effects, but we all rely on it to enable our income to meet our outgoings.

The list of criticisms of modern economic life is very long – from questions about money creation to proposals for localising trade. However, the program for yet more liberalisation and yet more innovation is equally long! Separating the two is a powerful but underestimated phenomenon – distrust of finance on the one side, near blind belief in its magic on the other. This is because we live in a time when finance – meaning money and capital – has become separate from social life, and the question is whether it becomes reconnected with humanity or strays apart. Our future depends on how we understand and overcome this problem.

The deciding factor is unlikely to be academic debate, ideological dispute, or even the vote. It will depend on what individual human beings do with their money – how they value it, trade with it, and use it as capital – and on the future basis we give to the unit of account, means of exchange, and surplus value functions of money. Events will become challenging indeed. Not just for us as private individuals, but wherever we find ourselves involved in and responsible for finance – whether as consumers, producers, policymakers, economists, bankers, fund mangers, or advisers. And whether in for-profit or not-for-profit organisations and in business, government, or humanitarian sectors.

The challenge we all face is to develop an *inherent* regulation of economic life that enables us to wake up in a realm in which for the most part we remain asleep. We need to show to ourselves that modern economic life does not have to be played out between anarchy and policing, which otherwise seems to be its fate.

What is the way forward? Is the solution to press on with capitalism in the hope that it will do more than just promise benefits for all? Is it to revisit socialism, notwithstanding the view of many that it has had its day? Or is it to find some third or green way? Or could it be that we need to metamorphose capitalism – by growing beyond its narrow preoccupation with the pursuit of self-interest, in the belief that invisible 'market forces' will create social order out of disparate acts, to enter a world that combines capitalist efficacy with genuine social inclusion born of conscious human action?

If we are to undertake such transformation, how are we to do so in practical ways that make sense in both micro and macroeconomic terms?[3] How are we to understand the global financial architecture, monetary policy, and the other 'big issues' that overarch our daily lives? And how *in our own circumstances* are we to manage change that of itself can reorient macroeconomic policies and attitudes?

---

[3] The associative economic meaning of micro-macro is discussed in the last chapter, *The World in our Deeds*.

2 Threefold Society

A key feature of modern times is that humanity is becoming responsible for the conduct of social life. In the past, this has been the task of gods, then priests, then kings, and latterly politicians. But now, as ordinary citizens – and indeed as ordinary mortals – we have to find our own way, the paradox notwithstanding that, while there can be no *one* way, our myriad paths have to cohere.

This paradox is a call to recognise that today's deep-seated need for human diversity and uniqueness, the 'driver' of so much individualism in our times, exists alongside an equally great need for universality and concerns in common – otherwise why care about what is happening in the world. The very term 'individual' says this, with its double meaning of both unique and indivisible. In the English language, this is expressed in that smallest of words, 'I', which refers to every one, even though none of us can call another by that name.

In similar vein, the human form is common

to us all, yet no two faces are the same. More fascinating still, every human being has three bodily 'systems' – nerves, respiration, and metabolism. The physical counterparts of thinking, feeling, and willing, they are never to be found in the same combination from one human being to another. This threefoldness is again reflected in modern social life, where much that otherwise appears confused and incomprehensible can look very different when one distinguishes between culture, politics, and economic life.

These insights, the last two of which come from Rudolf Steiner (see below and chapter five), have the great potential of providing human beings with reliable bearings at a time in human history that can otherwise be thoroughly disorienting. For who today does not find life bewildering? All manner of institutions and understandings are being uprooted, not to be replaced by arrangements of equivalent stability, but by experiments, fashions, and competing notions of what life is about.

Given such uncertainty, a longing can often be felt for order to be restored from outside by way of a single social conception. In reality, however, this cannot be a healthy development and will be possible only by imposition. Better, surely, for new order to be born of our own volition and diversity, and to be led in this way to those aspects of life that we have in common. For this, however, we need to create out of ourselves the stability that previously came from the past and from outside. This necessarily entails enormous uncertainty, which should not be glossed over or explained away with trivia.

Every human being today is undergoing in external social experience and without an obvious guide the kind of deep experiences that have always accompanied humanity, but which previously were experienced in special places (known as mystery centres), by relatively few people, and always in the presence of some authority. Central to this experience was 'the crossing of the threshold', an awakening to the fact that human existence has its 'roots' in a far deeper and wider reality than the physical world alone, an experience that engenders total doubt in oneself and the world, but is the key to opening oneself beyond the limitations of the single individual. Without this awareness, one was not fit to become responsible for the conduct of social life – not one's own and certainly not that of others.[4]

It is for these reasons that at the end of World War I, Steiner spoke in depth of the possibility of organising society as three autonomous spheres – culture, politics and economics – each self-governing according to distinct principles, yet cohering as a whole through the sovereignty of the individual human being and the fact that the individual is connected to all three and is thus able to reconcile their different logics. Steiner's overriding concern was to present the human being with a picture of society that at one and the same time responded to much-needed change, but also, because it was a reflection of the human being per se, served to orient him at this critical moment in history.

This picture of society is variously known in the English-speaking world as the threefold commonwealth, the threefold social order and the threefold state, or more simply as three-

---

[4] While outside the normal purview of economics, this is nevertheless a very important topic and one that is taken up more directly in *Step into Another World!* Associative Economics Institute, Canterbury, England and Neuchâtel, Switzerland, 2003.

folding. The original title of Steiner's book, however, was *Die Kernpunkte der Soziale Frage (Key Aspects of the Social Question).*[5] Written in 1917, its theme was the threefold nature of social life – not as a social scheme or political programme, but as observable reality. The approach was phenomenological, so that care should always be taken to try and see for oneself what he was referring to and to avoid treating the threefold idea as a slogan.

The Great War marked the time when, in Steiner's view, all external guidance had lost its validity, and a time when humanity was becoming caught up in a dangerous and false choice between the extremes of individualism and socialism (capitalism and communism). The threefold nature of social life provides an antidote to extremism in either direction. It is a social conception that sees both elements as necessary, but allows neither to predominate.

Individualism is a proper characteristic of cultural life; serving the needs of others is the proper principle of economic life. Between the

---

[5] Published in English: Rudolf Steiner, [1919]. *Towards Social Renewal.* Rudolf Steiner Press, London, 1977. A related publication is Rudolf Steiner, [1924]. *Threefold the Social Order.* New Economy Publications, Canterbury, 1996.

two, a third realm holds sway – one that is based on respect for one another and that provides the true foundation of equality and democracy. It is by recognising these phenomena and allowing them to become the organising principles of modern social life that human beings can combine the need for individualism with the equally powerful need to ensure the general well-being of humanity as a whole – to be co-responsible for our common wealth, in other words.

3 One-World Economy

The story being told here reaches its quintessence in modern economic life, especially modern finance, and the increasing experience of many that finance has become our master when it should be our servant. One sees this at its most rude in the idea that competition should govern all economic and financial affairs. For Steiner, however, competition more properly belongs to cultural life, in the sense of self-betterment, although, of course, this too has a powerful influence on economic life. Otherwise, when it comes to economic life human beings should cooperate to fulfil each other's needs, for it is in this, not in serving oneself, that each person will find his own true humanity.

Of course, modern social life seems far removed from this scenario. But is it? Is the competitive mode of economic life bringing the welfare that modern economists believe it will? According to the Oxford English Dictionary, competition in the modern sense has the opposite meaning of the Latin *competere*, "to strive for something together with another," a definition that makes association the true form of competition!

Without gainsaying economists' noble intent, have we not now had time enough to wonder at the reality of the idea that the pursuit of individual happiness promotes the well-being of all? Do not the wider features of modern life – especially today's increasing wealth disparities, which bring many other disparities in their wake – show that Adam Smith's 'invisible hand' argument, though alluring, is flawed and unreal?[6] Is the implication of the invisible hand true, for example, that human beings cannot be other than self-interested?[7]

The fate of Steiner's threefold commonwealth is interesting to consider at this juncture in history. It was intended to address

---

[6] "[The human being] intends only his own gain, and is in this, as in many other cases, led by an invisible hand to promote an end which was no part of his intention." Adam Smith, [1776]. *An Inquiry into the Wealth of Nations.* OUP, World Classics, 1993, Book IV, Chapter ii, p.292.

[7] Indeed, in an interesting article – 'Ethics and the Invisible Hand', Journal of Economic Perspectives, Spring 1993 – Jerry Evensky argues that at the end of his life Adam Smith considerably revised his view of human nature.

directly the many practical issues of the day, ranging from industrial relations to the gold standard – all problems that remain with us still. At the time, however, the victors of the Great War were too concerned to exact reparations from the German people, and any thought that German cultural life, in which Steiner's work was embedded, should have any say in world affairs was inadmissible. The depth of feeling on this matter, but also its flawed nature, is perhaps best appreciated by reading John Maynard Keynes's book written at the time, *The Economic Consequences of the Peace*,[8] in which Keynes, a key participant in the treaty negotiations at the end of World War I, points out the impossible scale of the reparations demanded and warns, accurately, of the consequences that would ensue were the German people to be so denuded of wealth and resources. Keynes was not heeded until the end of the 1920s, by when the Dawes and the Young Plans had reduced the reparations to the level he had originally suggested. By then, however, there had been a General

[8] J M Keynes, [1923]. *The Economic Consequences of the Peace.* Macmillan, London, 1971.

Strike in the UK, the Great Crash had occurred, and the events were in train in Germany that brought Hitler to power.

In 1922, in part because he saw where such developments would lead, Steiner added to his exposition of the threefold nature of social life, a further work – *Economics*[9] – in which he spelt out the way in which modern economic life would need to be based on the fact of a single world economy, treated as a common heritage by all the peoples of the world. In such an economy competition between nations becomes destructive and resources cannot be allocated by price alone.

Steiner was concerned to point out that economic life had become worldwide and that humanity needed to understand the importance of this, especially for the times we are now experiencing. Already then, the key question was whether the world economy was to be a shared affair or the prize and territory of only one nation? Was the world's wealth to become generally available or concentrated in a minority?

---

[9] Rudolf Steiner, [1922]. *Economics – The World as One Economy*. New Economy Publications, Canterbury, 1996.

In Steiner's terms, the choice facing humanity is clear and stark. On the one hand, there is the possibility of organising society as three autonomous spheres, a world characterised by a universal yet highly diverse cultural life born of the deeper tasks and capacities of human beings, by a multiplicity of polities predicated on mutual respect, and by a single world economy organised in the spirit and manner of global partnership. If not this, then a world will develop in which cultural life becomes ever more standardised and driven by consumerism, in which political life is dominated by power, empty phrases and broken promises, and in which economic life becomes a kind of fiefdom.[10] In such a world, the economy would become increasingly starved of fresh impulses and more and more the subject only of activities undertaken for the sake of a return to capital, rather than to meet human needs (albeit profitably).

This would be speculative and draconian language were it not a description of how things have turned out. For what has today's

---

[10] With its thesis that today's corporations are feudalist, Marjorie Kelly's book, *The Divine Right of Capital*, (Berret-Koehler, 2001) is interesting in this regard.

world become if not a great global economy, in which common wealth is a distant and foreign term? What have transnational corporations and financial markets become, if not soulless embodiments of enormous power capable of wreaking great havoc in social life and the source of deepening alienation? In both cases, institutions that in reality belong to a one-world economy have become distorted because our socio-economic constructs stop short of what today's development presupposes.

4 False Globalisation and the Sovereign Individual

But there is a further dimension to this. Steiner was concerned that if modern social life were not threefolded and based on a partnered world economy, there would come about a strong tendency to create, not a multiplicity of polities, but a single global polity with one world government. This, too, is not speculation. It is the avowed aim of many people, the merit of which and the techniques to bring it about can be found spelt out in many economic writings.[11] The path to this goal is seen to be first to create three polities, based on three currencies – the dollar, the euro and an Asian currency, currently the yen, but soon in all probability the Chinese currency. Beyond that lies a worldwide federation based on the US model.

In such a world, the state, not the individ-

---

[11] For example, Dani Rodrik, 2000. *How far will International Economic Integration go?* Journal of Economic Perspectives, Vol.14, No.1.

ual, would be sovereign. For those who champion human freedom this would be a tragic outcome, the result of accepting that competition and an invisible hand should rule economic life. In fact, these ideas will lead to the social failure of global competition, and it is this that will engender demand for a world government to sort out the resulting inequities.[12] The same ideas are already implicated in today's culture of sameness and a political life marked by lack of respect for the human being. The further thought, that economic life and thereby the wider reaches of social life are fashioned by the arbitrary working of market forces, only deepens the problem. For who has ever seen a market force? How can self-respecting, rational beings explain the entire working of the world by something that no one has seen or is ever likely to see? Worst of all, this view invites the notion of market failure,[13] requiring the state, and eventually global governance, to act as the regulator of

---

[12] See, for example, George Monbiot, 2003. *The Age of Consent – A manifesto for a new world order*. Flamingo, London.

[13] The failure of the market to produce or optimally distribute the goods required, to capture all costs (e.g. pollution), or to prevent monopoly.

human action since individuals cannot be trusted to act socially out of their own forces.

Today's globalisation is a false use of the fact of a single global economic life. 'False' for two reasons. First, because under current conditions the world economy is seen as some kind of international affair to be presided over and used by the more powerful nations, rather than as a single thing belonging not to nations but to humanity as such. Secondly, because this development is being experienced in a negative way – as something done to us and increasingly as something contrary to human well-being. In fact, the emergence of a single global economy is as huge and as cosmopolitan event as Alexander the Great's 'conquest' of the then known world; a bringing together of humanity as a whole.

False globalisation is giving rise to growing concern among millions of people, but it is met by force and by heads of state meeting at increasingly remote locations. For some people, of course, these are not problems, but the necessary 'pain' that must ensue as humanity adjusts itself to a market-driven social order. But for those who sense tragedy in train, this is not how the world should be evolving.

What, though, is the alternative? For many, it is to challenge globalisation with the power of civil society, to reinstate controls on global capital flows, and to insist that money issue is the prerogative of the state. These are uncertain and even dangerous alternatives, however. To the degree that they do not derive from the sovereignty of the individual but come more as a reaction to events, they will only lead to a strengthening of the current situation. In history, such reactions seldom escape the colour and tenor of the problem they seek to overcome, as the story of Marxist states illustrates well. To pass ownership of the means of production from one group in society to another, for example, does not change anything fundamentally. It merely changes who is in power.

The challenge, however, is not to change who is in power, but to overcome power as the basis of social life altogether. For this, humanity has to rely on the sovereignty of the individual, but this cannot come about unless and until power is set aside, outgrown.

5 Rudolf Steiner

The content and tenor of the previous chapters provide the necessary backdrop to understand the historical significance of associative economics. The reference to Rudolf Steiner is also part of this story and is likewise best made clear and explicit at the outset. A man of far-reaching insight, Steiner was born in Kraljevic, now in Croatia, in 1861. By the time he died, in 1925, he had become well known as the inspiration behind many practical endeavours, including 'bio-dynamic' agriculture, the Camphill curative homes and the Waldorf school movement. His role as an economist was less well-known, however, and remains so to this day.[14] There are many reasons for this, including the domination of economics by an Anglo-Saxon (meaning Anglo-American) approach, the perceived weirdness and 'impracticality' of what Steiner had to say (for example, that modern economic life

[14] But readers might like to consult *Rudolf Steiner, Economist*. New Economy Publications, Canterbury, 1996.

should be conducted independently of the state and not as a device of geo-politics!), his radical views concerning the manipulation of money, resources and markets, and the fact that he did not speak or write English.

More genuinely, to a large extent modern economics has set itself apart from a business or entrepreneurial interpretation of economic life, a development that has led it to adopt an increasingly mathematical formulation.[15] The result is that modern economics offers an abstract, even contrived, explanation of events, compared to which some would describe Steiner's approach as uneducated and unscientific.

Much depends, however, on how one un-

---

[15] Interesting in this connection, are remarks made shortly before his death in 1989 by Sir John Hicks, one of Britain's foremost economists in the twentieth century. Asked if he would like to be remembered as the accountant of the economics profession, Hicks replied, "I would not in the least mind… I have actually seen business decisions being made on the basis of projected balance sheets. I think that is the rational way to make a business decision. A lot of [today's] mathematical models, including some of my own, are really terribly much in the air…' Klamer, A., 1989. *An Accountant among Economists: Conversations with Sir John Hicks.* The Journal of Economic Perspectives, Vol. 3, Issue 4: 167-180.

derstands history (not to mention science!). Today's highly abstract explanations are accompanied by a troubled world that is in many ways the child of these abstractions. Creaking with uncertainty, both social and financial, modern life is riven by dangerous divisions that are not only social, such as the rich/poor divide, but also cultural – witness not only fundamentalist, but also moderate Islamic criticisms of western finance. Against such a backdrop, Steiner's observations have lost none of their relevance.

For example, Steiner saw the state's proper role as confined to the rights life – meaning the realm of relationships between human beings as such, the codes and laws by which they behave in regard to one another – and argued directly for it to let go its interference in cultural and economic affairs. Today, in contrast, the state permeates both these domains, creating unwieldy governance and obviating political, economic, and environmental responsibility on the part of individuals. Steiner also made much of the need to find a replacement for the gold standard, which was a major preoccupation at the time. For him, the answer lay in a differentiated concept of money, – in his terms, between purchase money, loan money, and gift money – which would have universal validity and provide not so much a world currency, as a world financial language. This differentiation reflects the standard view of money's three functions – means of exchange, store of value, and unit of account. Taken up later in this book (chapters 11, 15 and 16), such questions, remain central problems even now.

So central a reference to Steiner does not imply intellectual dependency. He is mentioned because of the relevance of his observations to so many aspects of associative economics, meaning the kind of economics that belongs to the economy when seen as a single global affair (not even as an agglomeration of national economies) and when conducted inclusively as regards humanity as a whole.

The aim is not to draw attention to Steiner *per se* or even to his work in a more general sense. It is to address a seemingly perennial problem in economics and one that Steiner also identified: the need for economics to give itself a real foundation in thought, meaning to think in accordance with worldwide metamorphosing processes, which it cannot do through the medium of the national, static concepts that currently permeate the whole of conventional economics. Such concepts are unsuited to today's reality – a matter considered further in the chapter on thinking associatively. We need a new approach.

6 Associative Economics

Having used the expression 'associative economics' many times already, it would be well to spell out its meaning, albeit at this stage only in a general way. Associative economics eludes precise definition; indeed, it goes with the territory that we need to describe and elaborate rather than define or prescribe what it means. The term is becoming widely used nowadays, by various writers and groups but with different meanings. In formal economics, for example, in the USA at least, it can refer to algebraic computation according to "associative laws", while Harvard's Department of Economics speaks of association as "independence of the order in which vectors are combined". There are psychological meanings also: from the University of California, "associative memory in connection with parametric estimation", and from Massachusetts Institute of Technology, "Brains are 'associative engines'. In cognition, association is about all we do."

A less cerebral use is that of Franco Archibugi, whose recent book – The Associative Economy[16] – was described by Jacques Delors as pointing to "the preservation of the Welfare State by way of its transformation into a Welfare Society." Paul Hirst uses the term 'associationalism'. More manageably, the US Green Party refers to an "associative sector [that exists] primarily for solidaristic rather than pecuniary reasons." In France, something of this social use of associative economics is also coming about. The French government, for example, recently appointed a Minister for Economic Solidarity, and there is a sizeable movement against neo-liberalism and maths-based economics. Here the emphasis is on the need for humanity to give new social meaning to modern economic life, to rediscover communitarian values and to shore-up society against the damage done by uncontrolled global financial markets. This use of the term seeks to maintain government and the nation state as the primary vehicle for socialising economic life. It is very uncertain, however, that the relentless logic of globalisation can be

---

[16] Franco Archibugi, 2000. *The Associative Economy – Insights beyond the Welfare State and into Post-Capitalism.* Palgrave Macmillan.

thwarted or redirected by a restoration of solidarity – by, in effect, re-regulating a de-regulated world. From the point of view of global finance, which is convinced that social order will follow upheaval in due course (that gain follows pain), solidarity is a retrenchment into socialism and definitely does not represent the future.

Then there are those who reference the term in the work of Steiner, whose role in this respect has already been discussed. For some time now, in Germany and in Holland, for example, there have been in existence a number of associative economic businesses taking their cue from the work of the economist Udo Herrmannstorfer, among others. Herrmannstorfer, in particular, has been the inspiration and driving force of many practical activities, ranging from food stores to pension funds, organisational policy to governmental advice. It is unfortunate that little of his work is available in English.[17] In America, the term is used to underpin community supported agriculture (CSA),[18] a movement with increasing presence

---

[17] But see Gaudenz Assenza, 1992. *Beyond the Market.* New Economy Publications, Canterbury.

[18] See, for example, Trauger Groh and Steven McFadden,

in the English-speaking world as people seek ways to befriend agriculture and to protect it from the ravages of a globalised free market.

In the Philippines, Nicanor Perlas, a third sector activist and champion of environmental and social causes, speaks of associative economics as the "economic arrangement, which fosters interaction among producers, traders, creditors and consumers, where appropriate price, true human needs, poverty eradication, equity, and impact on the environment are explicitly addressed in the process."

All these expressions convey the sense of a peripheral quality of thinking implicit in the term associate, as if people are sensing that economic reality is arrived at today by approaching it from a variety of perspectives rather than by self-assertion. If true, this provides an important insight into the meaning of associative, as distinct from competitive or market, economics, and may help characterise the difference between them. It shows, too, that associative economics is not a form of socialism: for socialism celebrates the state as

---

1997. *Farms of Tomorrow Revisited.* Biodynamic Farming and Gardening Association, Kimberton.

the key economic actor, whereas associative economics is about independent agents finding together solutions that meet their mutual interests when serving humanity.

As elaborated in this book, however, 'associative economics' has a further important nuance in that its focus is on making the meaning of economic relations explicit by way, among other things, of thorough-going transparency in finance and decision making and an emphasis on the need for the individual to take direct responsibility for modern economic life by applying such transparency to his own actions. Central to this view is the critical importance of human insight and the conscious use of will forces in determining outcomes that most people have come to believe proceed from economic, natural or historical forces, rather than human deeds as such.

In this sense, associative economics takes humanity beyond the market. In contrast to the lumbering nature of statism, the market may have much to contribute in terms of efficiency; but of itself it cannot generate the wider values that social and indeed economic stability rely on. These must be born from the will to create a social order in which the economy serves humanity, not the reverse.

Phenomenological in its approach, associative economics offers a wide perspective on today's economic life as the basis for an effective understanding of the many challenges we face, challenges that have both practical and moral aspects. It seeks a universal, rather than a merely western or market-centred approach to modern economic life. To this end it fosters cultural diversity, presupposes respect for the human being, and goes hand-in-hand with environmental sustainability.

With its many and wide-ranging implications for modern economic life, associative economics places human beings at the centre of all economic processes. Not in a sentimental or wishful sense, but because it is our capacity to be both free and responsible that enables us to make conscious what is otherwise left to the unseen working of market forces. As represented here, associative economics is cognisant of the wide ranging views that 'compete' to explain the workings of economic life – from Aristotle to Smith, Marx to Keynes and Friedman, as well as the 'sustainability critique' and the sophistications of modern finance. Its distinguishing mark, however, is that it is about individuals singly or together learning to take responsibility for their financial, social and physical environments by taking their contexts into account in carrying out what nevertheless remain the actions of free and responsible individuals. Associative economics is about not abdicating to governments or the market what properly should be centred in the human being.

7 From Competition to Association

This book is about the metamorphosis of capitalism. Put another way, it is about a transition from competition to association.

Competition drives modern economic life in two main ways: Firstly, when an individual or organisation competes against itself, with the economy benefiting from the improved efficacy resulting from honed skills and more precise relationships to customers. Secondly, when an individual or organisation competes against others to provide for human needs – usually under the auspices of achieving lower prices, although this is a contestable notion if one places the, often significant, indirect costs to the economy alongside the direct savings to consumers.

Paradoxically, perhaps, the second type of competition has the effect of rivals trying – and frequently succeeding! – to subsume one another. This type of competition impels increase in size – a process that knows no bounds and works, therefore, as a globalising force. This implies a serious problem of logic, however. Although most competition theory is predicated on the avoidance or socialising of monopoly, a global economy is necessarily increasingly monopolistic in character. In many cases, post-privatisation experience, for example, shows that fragmentation is often followed by consolidation, not only because of the intentions of providers, but *because the logic of global economics tends to monopoly*. At that point, the real issue becomes, not market domination, but ensuring that any gains resulting from monopoly are not made at the expense of, and are fairly distributed among, stakeholders generally. 'Stakeholders' is a wide and debated concept, however. To make it manageable, it is restricted here to mean principally investors (including bankers), suppliers, customers, personnel and the natural environment.

It is this phenomenon that will increasingly become the focus of understanding as economic life becomes more and more global. Under such conditions, the dynamic that results from one party competing against another becomes weaker, so that a new dynamic is needed. Thus, given the prevailing mindset, one can understand the continuation of *external* competition in the case of one organisation competing against another. *Internally*, however, simply in order to compete, an organisation has to pay attention to its synergies – removing overlaps, duplicated effort, and so on.

As the future unfolds, the second (but not the first) form of competition will increasingly give way to an economy of synergies. Within an airline, for example, money will not be made by delivering the fuel or food too late for take-off, but by delivering it in time to play its part in the larger enterprise. It is this shift from an external to an inherent dynamic that underlies associative economics, the need to form partnerships or to associate with other players in order to meet human needs. Associative economics thus offers a look over the horizon at the coming paradigm that will (or at least could) supplant the second type of competition.

Associative economics recognises the importance of solidarity – that is, of everyone being able to 'own' the working of economic life and to share in its fruits – but it does not accept that it is a task for government, still less the state, to manage or determine how this should be done. The essential role of government is to concern itself with the rights between human beings, and to this end to provide a context for economic conduct in areas such as health and safety. Associative economics renders obsolete the need for the state to socialise results because it sees this as a matter of deliberate practice on the part of economic actors, government departments included! In an associative economy, it is goes without saying that one has regard for the effects of one's actions on others and the world around one.

In this sense, associative economics is about higher egoism, about adding to one's own interests an awareness of the needs of others. It is a call to human beings to prove wrong those who argue that we are only able to think of ourselves and that to do otherwise is aberrant behaviour. This is the part that Smith left out in his early writings, but drew attention to in his later years.[19]

Crucially, associative economics looks to

---

[19] See Footnote 7, p. 26.

fairness in prices, whether these are the prices paid for goods, services, remuneration, or resources generally, and whether they are operating or balance sheet items. By 'fair' is meant that transactions are affordable to both parties, and that their effects are not rapacious or characterised by the false economics that short termism often, though not always, entails.

It is important to find ways – especially in regard to pricing – to effect a transition from competition to association; otherwise the risk is that modern economic life will become increasingly divided, not only in terms of North-South, rich-poor divides, but between neo-liberal and communitarian ideologies – the one continuing to argue that the needs of the wider community are best met by the pursuit of self interest, the other overlooking the role of the individual, believing him capable only of egotistical behaviour and therefore needing an external authority to compensate for his immaturity.

The need is to identify and/or devise ways to give effect to this transition, not only at the level of theory and policy, but in practical terms of taxation, profit distribution, internal governance, and so on. To this end, the associative approach provides a new way of looking at the world, not as an invented scheme, but as a perspective in which to assess existing and proposed ways of undertaking economic activity. It is not, however, a *prescription* of how people *should* behave, but a *description* of how they *could* behave differently. After all, the need to constrain economic life is not that at all. It is a need to constrain human selfishness.

8 Thinking Associatively

To a tidy mind, the variety of meanings ascribed to the term 'associative economics' in chapter 6 may pose a problem. And yet, market economics is not a uniform concept either. The point is that market economics reflects a centrist – more precisely, sense-based – way of thinking, which may have served us well as long as the underlying reality of modern economic life had not gone global, becoming all of one piece. But this kind of thinking is no match for the conditions of a single global economy, which is what we are now experiencing behind events, as it were; the more so since the gold standard was given up. Now we have to contend with what Keynes called a moving point rather than a fixed anchor, a reciprocator rather than a determinant, something that reflects back, rather than causes, the combined effect or net result of the myriad elements of economic life.

This means, however, that whatever arrangements we come up with and howsoever we describe new ways of doing things, the fulcrum of change is to think associatively. We need a new level of understanding. Addressing this problem, in his lectures on economics in 1922, Rudolf Steiner made an interesting observation. "The human brain weighs about 1400 grams. If you let this weight press on the veins and arteries at the base of the skull, it would destroy and kill the human being... [yet] the brain swims in the cerebro-spinal fluid and thereby loses 1380 grams. The brain only presses downward onto the base of the skull with a weight of 20 grams and this weight it can bear… With a brain, which was a mere ponderable mass, we could not think. We do not think with the heavy substance; we think with the buoyancy. The substance must first lose its weight. Only then can we think."[20] For this reason Steiner argued that to understand modern economic life we need to understand that we do not think with the brain, but with "that which flies away from the earth."[21]

Another way of understanding what he meant is to envisage that the kind of economics belonging to a single global economy is of

---

[20] *Economics,* op. cit., Lecture 1, p. 36.

[21] Ibid.

a higher order than market economics. "In economics we must speak of values, not goods, as the elementary thing. It is wrong to try to consider price in any other way than by envisaging the interplay of values... [When] you exchange value for value, price [arises as] *a fluctuating thing raised to the second power...*"[22] The reference is to price, but it can be generalised to associative economics in the same way that conventional economics is summed up in the one concept *'price-driven'*, essentially meaning that prices are determinative of economic conditions not following on.[23]

Put in more colloquial terms, associative economics requires the ability to think outside the box. But this is easier said than done. The

---

[22] Ibid., Lecture 2, p.49.

[23] The term 'price-driven' means to throw off external regulation of a cultural, moral or juridical nature, not in order not to be unregulated, but to become regulated by the price mechanism (market forces). In *Breaking Financial Boundaries*, Harvard Business School Press, 1991, David Meerschwam describes this most pervasive of influences in the viral terms of "infecting market after market."(95) The process is underpinned by a powerful argument: "Theoretically, in a purely price-driven world, various institutions offer similar products at similar prices. These prices, reflecting all available information about the product quality, result in an optimal allocation of all available funds." (104)

fact that we think inside the box is due to our acceptance of the many Enlightenment notions about human nature and the world that underpin and permeate the whole of modern economics. If we think inside the box it is because the Enlightenment removed from our credence any notions that man might have a higher or unseen dimension, that he might be connected to or descended from gods, or that he might have a spiritual side to his being. Deeper still, it is because we are a long way from Aristotle's day – that is, at the true dawn and with the true father of modern economics[24] – when the human being was understood to comprise body, soul and spirit. We long ago gave up the idea that man has a spirit; this happened in the 6th Council of Constantinople in 869. Then, with Marx, or rather with the materialist conception of history, the soul was jettisoned, so that by the time we entered the 20th century, we were well and truly left with only a body… and its equivalent in terms of economy theory – the labour theory of value. This is the explanation of economic life used

---

[24] In particular, in Book 5, Chapter 5, of Ethics, a seminal treatment of economics that even Marx refers to, see *Capital*, Vol.1 Penguin, London 1976, p.151.

by most people today, regardless of their position on the political spectrum and whether socialist or capitalist in their economic outlook.

To think outside the box, therefore, means to restore the element removed with the Enlightenment. Not by reinstating ancient teachings and understandings about the human being in his wider dimensions, but by rediscovering human spirituality in a completely concrete way through the medium of economic life, especially, as we shall see in later chapters, in connection with finance.

More formally, economics is a science of the invisible, in that no one has ever *physically* seen a price, a value, or inflation. We only see such things in thought. In this respect, it is not necessary for economic science to model itself on today's natural sciences. It need but identify axioms that have validity for the human being. But that means the human being has not only to be included, rather than excluded as a causative element; he is *the* cause of economic events. More radically still, he is the *only* cause. Economics can be attributed to nothing else. It calls to be predicated on the human being as such, not on 'laws' or 'cycles' or other supposedly objective phenomena.

Needless to say, this is a statement with extensive ramifications, which it is not intended to pursue, however. The aim here can be no more than to note the problem and its general consequences for modern economics.[25]

[25] A fuller treatment of this topic can however be found in this book's sister volume, *A Human Response to Globalisation*, see Footnote __.

9 Economics at a Threshold

To appreciate the case being made here for an associative approach to economic life, it is necessary to have some sense of the situation facing the discipline of economics itself, to which we usually turn when seeking to understand economic phenomena. Both in conceptual and practical terms, today's events have brought economics to the envelope of understanding that we call market theory, yet we do not have a clear idea as to what lies beyond this envelope. This process is leading (if it has not already led) economics to a critical point, at which, to paraphrase Keynes, it may well no longer be the case that economists, whether they are right or wrong, rule the world, or, to put it in detractors' terms, will continue to do so in an even worse manner than they have so far.[26] It will not do, however, to applaud the

[26] "The ideas of economists and political philosophers, both when they are right and when they are wrong, are more powerful than is commonly understood. Indeed, the world

implosion of economics: such an event would bring great suffering. Moreover, humanity urgently needs a mutually-agreed paradigm that we can all 'own' and that can also explain the next step in our economic evolution. In short, we need to transcend the threshold at which economics finds itself.

Speaking in Hong Kong in September 1997 about the danger of serious economic and social dislocation if markets are left to correct themselves, the well-known financier, George Soros spoke as follows. "I am firmly convinced that the present global capitalist system can be sustained only by deliberate and persistent efforts to correct and contain its deficiencies."[27] In an article he wrote at the time,[28]

---

is ruled by little else." J M Keynes, 1936. *The General Theory of Employment, Interest and Money*, Macmillan, London.

[27] For many people, it may seem contradictory to cite Soros, because of the predictable damage that can ensue when huge amounts of money enter and exit a market or country. The reference is not made to condone such behaviour, but to draw attention to the fact that someone intimately involved in, and therefore responsible for, such things is nevertheless able to critique them, and to do so to the extent of claiming that it is the financial markets, perhaps more than anything else, that are bringing economics to an impasse, exposing a serious contradiction, if not a fatal flaw in its reasoning.

Soros spelled out his critique of modern economic thinking more precisely:

"The main scientific underpinning of laissez-faire ideology is the theory that free and competitive markets bring supply and demand into equilibrium and thereby ensure the best allocation of resources.[29] This is widely accepted as an eternal verity and in a sense it is one. Economic theory is an axiomatic system: as long as the basic assumptions hold, the conclusions follow. But when we examine the assumptions closely we find that they do not apply to the real world.

"[In fact,] the assumption of perfect knowledge proved unsustainable so it was replaced by an ingenious device. Supply and demand were taken as independently given. This condition was presented as a methodological requirement rather than an assumption. It was argued that economic theory studies the relationship between supply and demand; there-

---

[28] *The Capitalist Threat.* Atlantic Monthly, February 1997.

[29] This is a reference to General Equilibrium Theory, which at its simplest turns on the idea that an economy comes to equilibrium when, in all markets, it is impossible to reallocate resources in order to make one person better off without thereby making another worse off.

fore it must take both of them as given. [Yet], the condition that supply and demand are independently given cannot be reconciled with reality at least as far as the financial markets are concerned.

"If the supply and demand curves are not independently given, how are market prices determined? [In] financial markets we find that, instead of tending toward equilibrium, prices continue to fluctuate relative to the expectations of buyers and sellers. [They] are not merely the passive reflection of independently given demand and supply; they also play an active role in shaping those preferences and opportunities. This reflexive interaction renders financial markets inherently unstable. Laissez-faire ideology denies the instability…"

Like Keynes, Soros is a rare bird in that he can explain his actions, while at the same time be 'successful' in the financial markets. Some people ask if it is valid for a market player to enter the realm of economic theory in this way. But the question, surely, is not whether he has a right to debate economic theory, or even that his own behaviour might be at odds with his reasoning, but whether his explanation has merit. Indeed, in America some time back, the 1991 Commission on Graduate Education in Economics warned of the danger of turning out "*idiots savants*, skilled in technique but innocent of real economic issues."

In *The Decline of Economics*,[30] the American writer, John Cassidy, speaks of economics as an "abstruse discipline that often appears to resemble a branch of mathematics." In its quest for rationality and utility,[31] "it is gradually becoming clear that the attempt to convert economics into an exact science has failed." According to Cassidy, we are not fulfilling 'the succession of Keynes', meaning that we are not solving the problem he sought to address of understanding how the economy works as a whole. This problem is especially crucial now that we are faced with the problem of a one-world economy pushing its way through an overlay of supposedly separate sovereign national economies.

Echoing Soros, Cassidy argues that the rational expectation ideas of the early 1980s, stemming from the influential economist,

---

[30] *The New Yorker*, 2 December 1996.

[31] That is, happiness, satisfaction.

Robert Lucas, rely on market theory. But "if the supply equals demand assumption is dropped, few of Lucas's conclusions hold up." Again, this is a reference to how, since World War II, economics has placed great store in general equilibrium theory, which purports to explain how all markets interact, but "these days [is] widely regarded as a splendid intellectual curiosity rather than as a model of reality."

In *The Crisis of Vision in Modern Economic Thought*,[32] Robert Heilbronner and William Milberg point to the need to include the "entirely human categories of purpose and will." For them, "as an existential metaphor, [rational expectations] was not acceptable [because] for all practical purposes, [it has] eliminated the individual himself… [All of which] presents ... economics with an unprecedented challenge ... the inescapable requirement [of regarding] itself as a discipline much more closely allied with the imprecise knowledge of political, psychological and anthropological insights than with the precise scientific knowledge of the physical sciences."

---

[32] *The Crisis of Vision in Modern Economic Thought.* Cambridge University Press, 1996.

Whether the 'soft' sciences are imprecise is perhaps a debatable point. They are probably better described as true to their own axioms. This, at any rate, is the challenge facing economics. As we saw in the last chapter, economics has reached a point where it needs to rest its scientificity on axioms that are true to its own nature. This is crucial if it is not to flunk the challenge before it by giving up its attempt to be a 'hard' science and falling into something less scientific. After all, 'physical' and 'exact' are not synonyms.

To help solve this problem, economics itself provides a great clue. Consider such terms as 'liquidity', 'inflation', 'growth', 'circular flow', 'currency', etc. Do they refer to a physical, mechanical world or one that is dynamic, even organic? Indeed, might its journey into abstruse mathematics not be a first, albeit crude, exercising of an inherent, but as yet unrecognised ability of economics to express this dynamism? If it could adduce self-supporting meaning from the phenomena it seeks to understand, it could outgrow the convenience of its marriage to mathematics.

10 Images

The ideas expressed in this book have more meaning than can here be elaborated, not only because they imply a radical rethink of economics as we know it, but because the landscape to which they refer is institutionally absent. Thus, to a certain extent, practical elaboration of these ideas lies in the future. In economics, however, especially associative economics, the future is all important. It is from there, not from the past, that economic life unfolds. It derives from what we do tomorrow, not from what we did yesterday.

If we can understand this, we will recognise that economics unfolds through our imagination of tomorrow; through speculation, if you will, in the sense of mirroring the future – as if one were able to hold a mirror above the horizon and see what is coming. Economics is thus image-dependent. In addition nowadays, whatever we imagine, we will enact. For this reason we need to be awake to the images we use. More than that, the quality of our images, and thus of the policies, institutions and events we give rise to, determines whether economics really is as dismal a science as is sometimes said or, as it could easily become, a radiant one. Indeed, right imagery is arguably the modern economist's first order of business.

The example of speculation is a case in point. The image just used – of a mirror above the horizon – is very different to the idea of robbery and deceit that many people use to explain the term. A second example is the reliance of economics on the earlier-mentioned vocabulary of circulation (liquidity, cashflow, etc.), which is a very positive image because it invites us to see we are part of a larger whole. In contrast, the image of the "invisible hand" is negative because, in allocating social responsibility away from the human being, it disempowers humanity, reducing human beings to 'noise', rogue elements that interfere with smooth 'objective' inquiry.

Another powerful image is in fact the sketch that appears in nearly every chapter of every economics textbook:

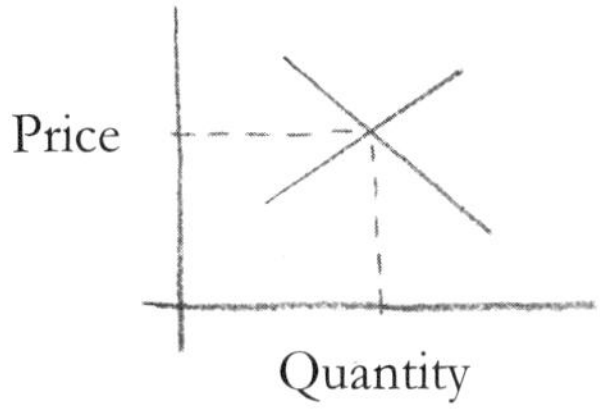

By means of this contrivance, conventional economics seeks to explain and organise the whole of modern economic life. But what is it? It is an image of how market forces are purported to determine everything and that the role of the human being, as regards economic activity, is to fit himself into the constraints of this construct. At this point, it matters a great deal whether one sees it as a stylised attempt to capture the nature of economic processes, as its inventors presumably understood, or takes it as gospel, as would an inexperienced youth in secondary school or university. But when taken as truth, as nearly every student and professor of conventional economics does today, then a harmless intellectual exercise becomes misleading and disorienting.

In contrast to this, consider two very different images (see below), that together provide a first step in articulating three important tenets if economics is to throw off its dismal reputation. Firstly, that a true economic science needs to evoke pictures that have shared and universal significance and that resonate in every human being. Secondly, that economics is capable of visual expression that is more alive and real than the usual dry imagery associated with its dismal version. Thirdly, that economics needs such imagery if it is to become something that all cultures can 'own', that respects traditional value-systems, and that takes it beyond the epithetical charge of being only western and skewed in favour of Anglo-American interests.

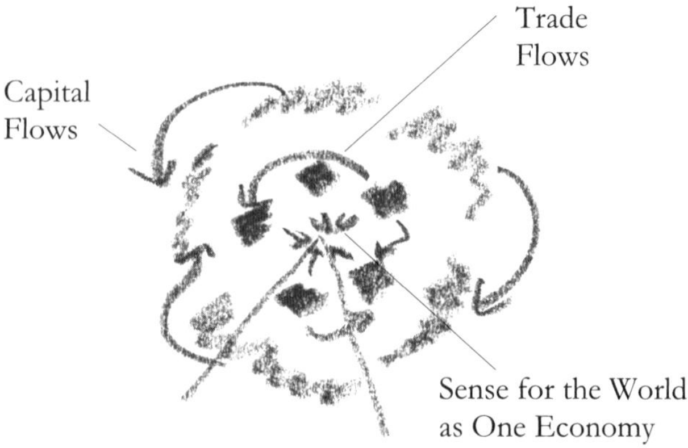

Individual Activity in a Global Context

The first image is meant to convey a number of themes already discussed. Firstly, that modern economic life is based on a single global economy, for which the sketch as shown here could be a proxy, with the five segments representing the continents. But it could also be five countries or five provinces, five companies or five departments. Or it could be five different types of activity, e.g. a hotel, church, post office, school and factory. It is important to note that in this image, no particular significance is given to business, government or civil society, for these are political rather than economic distinctions. The point is to illustrate that what matters is the way they are related to one another – how capital and trade flows between them and whether they have an awareness that they belong to a larger economic context.

Epistemologically, global does not just refer to our ability to understand individual action in its larger setting. To think globally and act locally means to become aware of the wider context and effects of individual economic actions and to realise that one only achieves something because one has partners ranging from clients to investors, suppliers to auditors.

The second image has three elements and is used several times in this book. Its purpose is to show three things: (i) that threefoldness is a frequent phenomenon of economic life and can be taken as a true given; (ii) that this threefoldness has a further dimension in that one of the elements is of a higher order than the other two; and (iii) that by approaching them in this way, the human being is oriented in 'economic space'. By its means he can get his bearings in regard to the central issues of our times and feel himself part of their solution.

11 Accounting and Accountability

Images on their own are not enough to bring economics into an associative landscape. They are, so to speak, what the right brain needs. The left brain needs something more precise, concrete and calculable – something that conventional economics has long sought and tries to emulate in its quest to be scientific and its assumption that this can be met by statistics and mathematics. The latter appeals especially to our need to give economics ostensible objectivity. After all, we cannot organise a global economy on subjective notions. There is too much at stake.

In associative economics this quantitative aspect, with all that can follow from it in terms of objectivity and ineluctable logic (so-called laws) is found in accounting.

At the risk of labouring the point, this is why accounting has such an emphasis in associative economics in the sense meant in this book. As the language of finance, accounting provides for measurability at the same time as it acts as a medium for developing true economic consciousness.

It would take us too far afield to discuss why, towards the end of the 19th century, economics parted company with business and 'cycles' took the place of balance sheets. Suffice it to say, that the earlier reference to Sir John Hicks is important. The crucial thing to understand is that the need for economics to be scientific and for it to ground itself in global realities, needs the combination of appropriate images and clear accounting. Accounting, because it possesses a wisdom that human beings can rely on, if they would but recognise it and allow it to shape their economic activity.

Simply stated, accounting is constructed of three elements, thus:

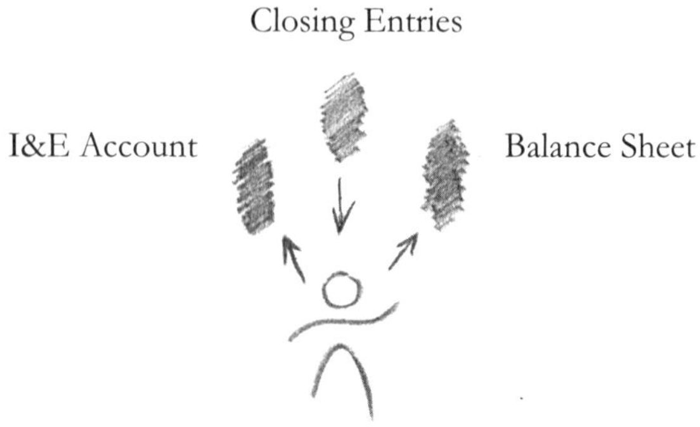

Of these three, one is of a higher order in that it is known through its effects as they appear in the other two. The choice of a depreciation rate, for example, shows up in and strongly influences the income and expenditure account and the balance sheet.

This logic or structure is worldwide, but it is by no means always recognised. Governments, for example, do not have balance sheets, many not-for-profits do not take them seriously, and many companies use accounting selectively for reporting to the tax authorities or to shareholders (not to mention for fraudulent purposes!), rather than for revealing the reality of their situations.

Much more could be said on this matter and it is indeed touched on elsewhere in this book. But the purpose of this chapter is only to draw attention to the enormous importance of accounting and the logic that underpins it. When one understands accounting in this way, it yields two further dimensions that are vital to the associative economics story. It is no accident that accountability shares its etymology with accounting. Thereby, it provides the very medium for public bodies – for-profits, not-for-profits or governments – to make visible what they do on behalf of society. For example, it is said that a central bank like the European Central Bank is democratically in deficit because its unelected officers are a law unto themselves. Yet their task is not one that can be carried out just because one is elected: one needs expertise, financial expertise. And the best way to make such expertise transparent is through accounting, meaningfully constructed, diligently maintained, and openly reported.

At the same time, accounting is the language of finance. If we were all to track our activities in accordance with the logic of accounting we would find we had a common language.

Lastly, to maintain and report clear detailed and open accounts requires huge effort of will, meaning, as described in chapter 8, the discovery of afresh of human spirituality. Accounting is the medium for doing this, which is why false accounting is the main means for obfuscatory reporting and for concealing the true nature of one's activity from the rest of humanity.

12 Making the Invisible Hand Visible

So far in this story much reference has been made to a central tenet of associative economics – the need for human beings to become conscious of economic processes and to collaborate deliberately to bring about a healthy economic life, both in terms of its own workings and its effects on society. This is simply the culmination of the backbone phenomenon of history, the process of individuation.[33] On the face of it, therefore, this is a straightforward and historically real proposition.

In fact, it is by no means easy to achieve because individuation has an important corollary. It calls on human beings to be responsible for their own destinies and to engender directly the many social and economic processes that we have become used to regarding as the responsibility of others, especially governments and experts in finance,

[33] The process leading to or the condition of being an individual. – Oxford English Dictionary.

such as accountants, bankers, economists and so forth.

In macrosocial terms, conscious will is about freedom *and* responsibility. It is far easier to be free, in the sense this is usually meant today – free to do as one wishes – than it is to accompany freedom with responsibility. Constraining one's actions so that their effects are benign, for example, takes a lot of effort. It takes will forces to stop always seeking a low price, to buy products that have not been made by child labour, or to avoid 'unethical' use of one's savings.

In this matter, two things are important to emphasise from an associative point of view. The first is, that, not only is it hard work to take hold of one's will forces and to direct them towards a greater good than just one's own interests; in doing so one is going against the grain of modern economic life insofar as the thoughts and policies that shape it, as well as the instruments we use on a daily basis (pensions, savings, shares, etc.), are all predicated on such notions as an invisible hand and market forces. Children of the Enlightenment, these ideas are underpinned by some very powerful conceptions concerning free will and democracy. Is the human being free, for example, and what is proper governance for our times?

It is not for nothing that modern economic life is also causing great change in the political landscape – witness the use of the euro to turn Europe into a political entity, Britain's casual but far-reaching review of its constitutional make-up, or the pressure on Switzerland to change not only its laws and economic customs, but also the special genius that informs them, by, in effect, giving up being Swiss. It is not for nothing, either, that the two powerful conceptions in which associative economics is embedded challenge those of the Enlightenment – the idea that economic life is one of three distinct but interdependent spheres in society, and the image of economic life having gone global and having no jurisdiction less than the world as a whole. These differences will come increasingly to the forefront in the years ahead. Already people are saying that a world economy needs a world government, yet the threefold idea would go in a different direction: although the world economy needs to be managed as a global affair, political life should stay country-based.

These matters are mentioned because they all weigh heavily on the human being in that they require great forces of will if they are to be understood and if we are not to take wrong turnings in history. It needs forces of will even to think about such things, certainly to think them through. But it needs even greater forces of will to act them out, the more so if 'majority opinion' seems bent on going in a different direction. One could say much more, but the point is simply to alert the reader to the fact that modern economic life, and associative economics in particular, places great emphasis on the need for individual human beings to become conscious of their will forces and to give them direction out of their own volition, not out of duty or because governments or experts tell them to do this or that.

In a word, associative economics is about making the invisible hand visible. Smith's contrary suggestion notwithstanding,[34] it is

---

[34] The keystone of modern economics is Smith's condemnatory remark that "...to narrow the competition is always in the interest of the dealers, ...an order of men ... who have generally an interest to deceive and even to oppress the public, and who accordingly have, upon many occasions, both deceived and oppressed it..." *Wealth of Nations*, op. cit., 1; xi, p.157.

about making clear that we will not achieve a healthy economic life unless we deliberately cooperate to that end, denying to ourselves the excuse of automaticity that market forces implies, and making ourselves the agents for the many processes that we are normally wont to place outside ourselves. It is about proving that when human beings cooperate in economic life this is not by definition collusive behaviour. That depends on the how and what of their collaboration. Of course, people can get together to corner a market or to deny information to others. But they can also get together to raise money for those in need – witness *Live Aid, Medicins Sans Frontieres,* and a host of other humanitarian activities. The difference is that the former has no higher purpose in mind, it is simply self-serving; while the latter is inconceivable if it were not undertaken for some noble cause that benefited others. One would simply not be able to access the forces needed if one were only thinking of oneself.

The second feature of associative economics in this regard is the recognition that the human being cannot make this step in history if the ideas, policies and institutions he creates do not reflect and reinforce an awakening to the reality of human will. More than that, they need to enable us to recognise this element as fundamental and equip us to manage it. One says colloquially, "Where there is a will there is a way." Just so, one can equally say, "Where there is a way, the will has no excuse, the will can follow." It is vital not to underestimate the effect on human will of not enacting what one knows should be done or what one knows to be true. This effect can be one of stasis, of giving up, and thence of deferring to outside agencies.

If we are to build an economy out of sovereign individuals we must simply add to our self interest the next stage in our development – higher egoism, service to a greater whole, an awareness that each individual economic act belongs to the global economy and has its meaning in that context. We must learn that the 'building blocks' of a global economy are the myriad actions of sovereign individuals, countless actions by countless human beings the world over every day. But we must also recognise that Smith has a real point if the actions that proceed from sovereign individuals do not contain within them an image of the global economy. They need to be in themselves microcosmic expressions of that economy.

In America, one uses expressions like 'walk the talk' and 'building the road we travel'. These are will expressions.[35] With the particular eloquence of the street, they tell about the need to avoid discrepancy between what one knows to be right and what one does, and the fact that from here on human beings have to create their world out of their own actions and out of their own value systems. They – that is, we! – also have to do these things in mutual respect. Our disparate actions have somehow to unite in a viable whole, not by way of some unseen deity knitting them together, but through respect for one another, by recognising our diversity, by capitalising one another's initiatives, and by deliberately collaborating to ensure we all enjoy economic well-being, but without this meaning sameness as regards income or wealth. The problem here is not differentiation. Indeed, the difference in in-

---

[35] America is above all a country of will forces. Indeed, one understands much about the United States when one understands how difficult it is to manage this aspect of human existence.

come and wealth levels is an important dynamic in economic life. The problem is that the disparities are too great and that one end of the spectrum entails poverty, while, at the other, money as such is often the basis of power – an attribute that comes not from money but from the selfish side of human nature.

Action that would be at once practical and ethical can only originate in the human being. One could even go so far as to say that it is only if we are able to act in this way that we can beget the very forces of will such action requires.

A key part of associative economics is thus the part it can play in helping human beings undertake economic activity in the light of such huge, yet everyday, historical and philosophical considerations.

13 Revelatory Economics

The theme of cohering will forces entails two others, each of which is crucial to our understanding of associative economics and in a sense provides a test to see if its spirit has been recognised.

The first concerns our notion of money – whether it is a thing in itself, as conventional economics assumes, or representative of processes we otherwise cannot 'see' (and thus become aware of). To pass into an associative economic landscape necessarily entails passing through the eye of this particular needle. For, living deep in our souls, it is our belief that money is a thing in itself that feeds the main financial feature of our times – the phenomenon of faithless global capital working through the world's financial markets, or, as Steiner put it, the fact that 'money is now doing business on its own account.'[36] Under today's

[36] *Economics,* op. cit., Lecture 9.

conditions of abstract finance, it is not only the idea that money is a thing unto itself that is at 'fault', however, but also the fact that thereby the human being absents himself from financial and monetary processes. Financial markets then *appear* to be abstract or remote, but this is not quite the truth. More accurately, they seem thus because they lack the 'presence' of the human being.

If we would ground modern finance in a truly responsible way, therefore, we have to insert the human being at its every stage and moment and for this we need an appropriate medium. By integrating ourselves – that is, by cohering our will forces – the world of finance will in turn lose its abstract quality. Not tomorrow, for it did not become abstract just yesterday, but as the start of a long process reaching as far into the future as the present level of abstraction leads us back into the past.

The second has to do with how consciousness is built, at least as regards economic phenomena. This is inwardly related to the first because to speak of consciousness raising or cohering will forces is to look at the same thing from two directions. It is about taking will into thinking or thinking into will. In other words, consciousness is built by entering into contrasting experiences and resolving any contradictions, tensions or dilemmas that arise. The world becomes known by dividing it into two, then knitting it back together again out of one's own being.

Examples of such contrasts in this book are:[37]

Images	Accounting
Production	Savings
I&E Account	Balance Sheet
Tangible	Intangible
Goods	Culture
Micro	Macro

Moreover, by differentiating between two aspects and discerning their distinct logics, the individual becomes sensitised to a third element – not his own thoughts or intentions, to which conventional economics gives emphasis, but his ability to go behind both and to 'listen' for the deeper significance of what he thinks and what he does, his intentions and his actions. By coming out of the enclosing nature of self interest and exercising his capacity for

[37] Note: The list is not analogical.

higher egoism, the individual is able to see himself from the global economic point of view. Neither he nor his actions are any the less individual thereby. Rather, they become suffused with awareness of their larger significance.

In this way, one becomes aware of what the single global economy would have one do. To the attuned individual, the requirements of the single global economy reveal themselves and the 'right' thing to do becomes apparent. This takes further what is meant by saying that one element is of a higher order than the other two.

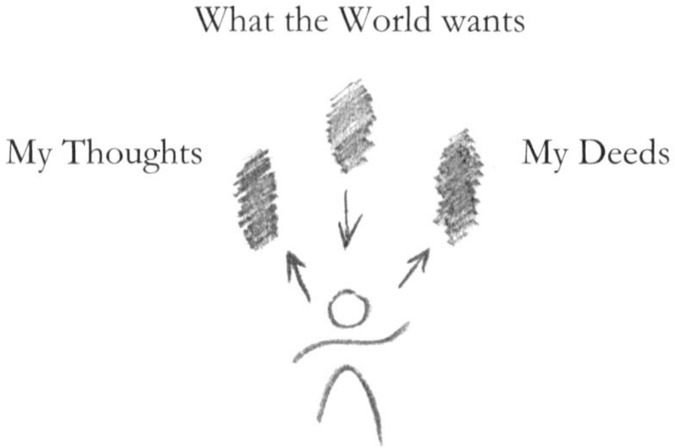

In this sense one can speak of revelatory economics, the shadow of which we know today as market forces and the invisible hand, but which in a conscious economic landscape would simply be the harmonious collaboration of sovereign individuals, cohering their will forces to achieve stable and inclusive economic conditions for humanity as a whole.

14 Doing Business Associatively

Having set forth many of the considerations that underlie associative economics, this chapter outlines an associative way of doing business.

To begin with, it is important to define some terms. Firstly, as will be evident from what has been said in earlier chapters, associative economics is predicated on and provides a medium for the individual to act on behalf of humanity's economy as a whole. Key to this is the need to have capital at his disposition through which he can exercise responsible initiative. In doing so, he becomes responsible for the capital and for linking it to the world economy through how he uses it. In this book, such a person is called an entrepreneur.

Secondly, the term economic activity (more generally, business) is generic and applies to any activity in which individuals singly or together do something for others, whether the activity is agricultural, industrial, commercial, financial, governmental, humanitarian or cultural, and regardless of its size, locality and domain of operation. This is a carefully considered formulation: while it recognises the different nature of economic activity as between governments and businesses, for example, it does not follow the model of saying there are two main types – or even three, if one adds humanitarian organisations (NGOs). Associative economics is predicated on human beings being responsible for economic activities of a whole range, from hospitals to cinemas, schools to factories, banks to government agencies. The differences lie in what they do: nursing or financing, selling food or shipping. Otherwise, they are all of one type insofar as an economic activity can be defined as any undertaking in which human beings meet the needs of other human beings and do so profitably.

Profit can be a controversial subject. Not for financial people, of course; nor, if they are awake, for investors, whose earnings depend on it. But among many critics of modern economic life, profit is a dirty word – referring to something that should not happen or, if it does, should not be privatised but should accrue to the public benefit in some way (but usually via the Treasury!).

This is a somewhat political approach, however. From an *economic* point of view, profit is akin to the air we breathe. Without it economic activity cannot respire. In an associative economy, the concern is always that the profitability of an enterprise should derive from 'right' behaviour. The real question is whether the profit is calculated before or after the true costs of an activity have been met, including in particular any costs it avoids by passing them onto society's balance sheet, underpaying people, cheating customers or destroying nature. If an activity has had no negative impact on its social and physical environments, there is little economic reason to begrudge it its profits.

In this connection, it should not be thought that a not-for-profit does not make a profit. Its accounts show otherwise. The difference between a for-profit and a not-for-profit is twofold. Firstly, income in the first is sales, in the second donations. Secondly, profits in the first belong to and are distributed among the investors, whereas those in the second belong to and are retained for the purposes of the organisation.

Indeed, a key part of the associative approach is that the classic distinctions between for-profits, not-for-profits, and governmental agencies disappear. As meant here, therefore, associative economics is not a tri-sectoral approach. Rather than bringing different sectors together, its emphasis is on each and every activity having the same archetypal profile as regards its structure and accounting, regardless of whether it adds value by opera or coal mining, teaching or retailing. Here, 'adding value' means meeting needs through the uniqueness of one's contribution, through the skills and gifts one has to offer society. Through, in effect, an associative version of comparative advantage.

In conventional economics this term originates with David Ricardo (1772-1823) and means "the idea that economic agents are most efficiently employed in activities in which they perform relatively better than in others."[38] Today the term tends to be overshadowed by *competitive* advantage, which is

[38] Penguin Dictionary of Economics, 1992.

not at all the same concept.[39] In the Ricardian sense, comparative advantage has a marketised, transaction-driven nuance, but in associative economics this nuance disappears and the concept moves to the pole of uniqueness – of the gifts and destinies of individuals and even whole peoples. Brazil ceases to be a potential market for lending or selling into or for extracting raw materials and cheap labour from. The question ceases to be how can Brazil, or any other country, produce the same things as anyone else but more cheaply. It becomes: What does Brazil have to offer humanity as a whole that is uniquely Brazilian? For it is this that one would seek to finance in an associative economic world. We are not concerned with a price-driven race to the bottom (even if that is no-one's intention). In associative economics the aim is not low prices for the sake of it, but prices that can be afforded by both parties to any transaction, prices, that is, that allow each party to remain in profitable operation. For this to work, however, the key concept is that of a choir of

---

[39] 'Competitive advantage' derives from Michael Porter of Harvard Business School's Institute for Strategy and Competitiveness.

peoples. The differences in level implicit in human diversity provide the key dynamic in an associatively-conducted single global economy. This is the new, or at least, associative economic meaning of comparative advantage.

The archetypal approach to economic activity (or business) has the further implication that, when it comes to finance, while the field of endeavour may vary and thus give specific nuances or colouring to an activity, the fact that they belong to a single global economy requires them to speak one language, namely, the language of finance – accounting (see chapter 11).

For this reason, in the sense meant here, an associative economic business tracks itself through a clear set of income and expenditure accounts and a balance sheet. Whether it belongs to corporate life, government or civil society, they all come onto the same page, maintaining detailed up-to-date and transparent accounts. It is the fact that governments do not have balance sheets and that not-for-profits tend to be spenders rather than makers of money that gives corporations such power today. This power derives in large part from the fact that corporations are, relatively speaking, financially conscious. That said, they are often by no means as financially conscious as one might imagine or expect, even before one mentions the cases of fictional and fraudulent accounting. Suffice it to say, that creating a level playing field through accounting and finance is not a way of 'corporatising' the world. It is a way of bringing all kinds of economic activity into the same room, as it were, getting them to speak the same language. This will be a challenge for all three types of organisation – business, government and third sector. As such it is the macroeconomic aspect of the will question discussed in chapters 12 and 13.

This emphasis on finance is crucial because associative management of economic life is mediated by finance, in the sense that finance provides a universal language, valid in all domains, whether a self-employed individual or a corporation, a government department or a volunteer organisation. Finance is the great mediator. In a truly global economy, it is not national trade balances that matter, but, poverty excluded, the differences in levels of income and wealth (money and capital). For this dynamic to become visible and brought into play we need to use finance because it provides a technical means to identify and manage our will forces, working with which is the 'substance' of associative economics.

To understand the dynamic operation of such a conception, it is essential to place the sovereign individual at its centre, for it is his recognition of the threefold nature of society and economic life alike (discussed in chapter 2), and his respect for and refusal to conflate the different logics of their three aspects that ensures they do not become confused and that none of them seeks to determine the others. To reiterate the threefold thesis: Society has three distinct aspects (culture, politics and economics), each managed autonomously in accordance with its own logic, yet all three cohering as a whole through the fact that the individual human being is common to all.

Under today's conditions, the counterpart to this – itself an expression of the autonomous conduct of economic life – is that every economic activity is also in a certain sense sovereign. It is the key to successful financial management that the three elements of which a business is comprised – aim, management and capitalisation – are held in a coherent, unconfused relationship. Otherwise those responsible for it will not be able to listen out for, and thus hear, the intuition the business expresses and seeks to realise.

For this reason, the structure of an activity needs to provide a context that is appropriate to and compatible with the listening element on the part of those responsible for it. The legal and other arrangements by which an economic activity is organised can and will vary, depending on the number of people involved, scale of operations, product or service offered, and the constitutional genius of the country it operates in. Speaking in this way does not prescribe what such arrangements shall be in detail, but points to the archetypal or generic aspects that need to be considered if capital is to be linked to a real intuition. A comprehensive (if somewhat convoluted!) way of capturing the essence of this is to say that an associative economic business is structured so that its existence as a legal person, the management of its activities, and the financing of its means of production are distinguished from each other, in order that no one element has undue power over the other two. In particular: its aim and existence are independent of both the providers of the finance for its means of production and of the views and opinions of its management, its financing structure guarantees its long term independence, and it is managed in a clearly documented and transparent manner.

A final consideration is the need for an associative economic business to use its accounts in a way that only makes sense if one understands finance as a way of becoming conscious of the coherence of one's activity with the wider economic world. In this regard, it is important to meet on a regular basis with fellow associative economic entrepreneurs for the sake of sharing financial information as between peers, rather than as required for reporting to investors or the tax man. Two key elements in this meeting are the peer dialogue that then ensues and the need to make a global picture of the otherwise separate activities involved. These are crucial elements because they provide a praxis for the two aspects of associative economics deemed most important – the need for those responsible for an economic activity to access the intuition it belongs to and the need to take account of the fact that one's context is the global economy.

Both these elements make concrete what is meant by higher egoism and cohering one's will forces, considerations which are in fact two sides of one coin. Neither makes any sense if one is only concerned with one's own interests, of course; but that is their point. They have meaning only if one wishes to cross the threshold at which humanity now finds itself. They belong to the next dimension of economic life, the landscape of associative economics, into which they provide a gateway.

To speak thus is to iterate precepts, of course, to set down guidelines for assessing 'associativeness'.[40] This is deliberate. However, while archetypes can be formulated in the abstract, their very universality means that how they express themselves in any particular instance cannot be prescribed. Thus, an associative economic business could take any number of forms – corporate or governmental, for-profit or not-for-profit, cooperative or company – but it will bear the stamp of the

---

[40] Indeed, these guidelines are expressed more formally in the ⓐⓔ Quality Guarantee Mark, a unique scheme established in 1998 in which an associative approach to modern economic life as been 'embedded' in a set of explicit criteria – visit www.ae-institute.com.

same archetype. Associative economics necessarily involves the paradox of universality on the one hand and diversity on the other.

15 Differentiated Money

Returning to the big picture, in these final chapters we return to the wide panorama of an increasingly divided world overshadowed by financial markets of uncertain stability and blighted by totalitarianism, on the one hand, and righteous neo-imperialism, on the other. How can all that has been said so far have any possible impact on the big issues that race ahead of 'small' history, and which, because of their inherently threatening quality, give constant encouragement to survivalist self-interest? How can higher egoism enter world affairs at the 'macro' level?

The answer to this lies in looking more closely at the implications of accounting and finance, in the associative economic sense explored earlier (chapter 11). It is interesting to note that textbook descriptions of money describe it as having three functions: as a medium of exchange (MX) for effecting payment for goods and settlement of debts and other contractual obligations; as a store of value (SV) for holding wealth; and as a unit of account (UA), providing a numeraire for quoting prices and keeping accounts.[41]

Although by no means as well-known, equally interesting is Steiner's concept of three kinds of money, introduced in chapter 5, in which he speaks of 'purchase money' (PM), 'loan money' (LM), and 'gift money' (GM) – meaning respectively money used for consumption, money used for investment (more precisely, the financing of the means of production), and money spent on the development of the individual and even a whole people (education in the most general sense). This last is of particular importance: Gift money is money that is needed by neither trade nor capital, and which is best used when donated to those people or institutions that comprise cultural life, on the grounds that for society generally it represents an ever-renewing source of new ideas and talents from whence new values flow.

Now, it does not require much thought to

---

[41] A fourth function – money as a standard of deferred payment – is often mentioned, but this is really a subset of the unit of account function.

see a similarity, at least, between three *functions* of money and three *kinds* of money:

MX – Exchanging Goods and Services – PM

SV – Capitalising Enterprises – LM

UA – Funding Culture and Education – GM

Whether these terms are analogous in the strict sense need not be a matter for now.[42] The point is that they allow each set of terms to be evaluated anew, giving more qualitative meaning to the functionalism of conventional economics at the same time as linking Steiner's terminology to known contemporary vocabulary.

But the story goes farther. The global financial architecture (trade, capital and central banking) also has three elements. So, too, as noted earlier, does accounting (income and expenditure accounts, balance sheet and closing entries).

Finally, in the sense explained earlier, one of

---

[42] In fact, they are not direct analogies. It is more that, as threesomes, they have equivalence and reiterate the threefold structure of socio-economic life. The analogy passes through the individual, who is common to all cases.

the three is of a higher order than the others: closing entries are 'above' income and expenditure accounts and the balance sheet, as gift money, unit of account and central banking are 'above' purchase and loan money, means of exchange and store of value, and trade and capital.

If only as a device, it is interesting to consider the similarity of these different threesomes:

Closing Entries
Gift Money
Unit of Account
Central Banking

I&E Account
Purchase Money
Means of Exchange
Trade

Balance Sheet
Loan Money
Store of Value
Capital

Representing them in this way suggests they are indeed inter-analogous. Moreover, if one bears in mind the idea, central to associative economics, that accounting is a constant matter regardless of the size, scope, or domain of an activity, that finance is a universal language, and that all activities, whether business, government or third sector, need to come onto the same page, then one can see that accounting has a special significance. Transposed into the three other versions of economic analysis, the logic it obeys at the micro level is equally valid at the macro.

In other words, if we organise our economic activity according to the logic of accounting we are organising it in universal, global terms. Thus, accounting is the key tool for giving every individual access to the big problems of our time. It provides us with a medium for discharging our historical responsibility, denying us the excuse of being 'little people'.

16 Beyond Gold

That accounting is crucial to economic awareness is an observation pregnant with consequences for today's world, which operates on a global scale and is driven (or so we say) by footloose global capital working through financial markets. For there is one 'event' above all that faces modern humanity – in a global economy there can be only one currency. Lurking within current events, this problem comes down to a simple question: What is to replace the US dollar as the world's reserve currency? Two main scenarios can be envisaged. The first, a militarised dollar (for the US is not keen to give up its hegemony, if for no other reason than 85% of its dollars are outside the USA[43]). Second, a threesome of the dollar, the euro and the yuan, leading in due course, presumably, to a single, albeit articulated, global denomination. Something

---

[43] According to a foremost world authority, Robert Mundell, in *The International Monetary System in the 21st Century*, lecture delivered at St Vincent College, Letrobe, Pennsylvania, 12 March 1997.

along these lines is already happening in the form of the zones' respective central banks holding each other's currencies as reserve currencies – though with the yen not (yet) displaced by the yuan.

But these remain fiat currencies. Behind them is the deeper question, therefore: should we not return to gold or in some other way re-establish world finance on the basis of a universal currency, free of political interference?

In its detail, this is too big and complicated a subject for this book, involving the intricacies of *n*-1 exchange rate theory, central bank independence, monetary policy, and much else. It needs to be addressed even so, for without it we cannot get a true measure of the relevance of associative economics for our times.

In one respect, in particular, one can observe a resonance and even consonance of ideas as between Steiner and Keynes, both men writing in the early 1920s. In his lectures given in the summer of 1922,[44] Steiner refers to the need to replace the gold standard with economic management based on three kinds

[44] *Economics*, op.cit., especially lecture 12.

of money and on the further concept of money as global bookkeeping.[45] His point was to find a next step after the gold standard, which, for all that can be said against it, had come to operate as a quasi-global currency prior to its suspension at the outbreak of World War I.

In his *Tract on Monetary Reform*,[46] Keynes pondered the same question. Published in 1923, this is a complex text and any detailed exposition of it would be out of place in a book such as this.[47] What can be shared is an image, which, while admittedly an interpretation, serves well to illustrate Keynes's essential thesis.

---

[45] Describing money as a token, rather than a thing in itself, that parallels the production, distribution and consumption of values in the economic process, Steiner says, "Truly we may describe money essentially as a kind of book-keeping system for the whole world economy… When some item is transferred or delivered, this simply signifies its entry in another place. The thing is done by passing money … form hand to hand [but] the principle is fundamentally the same … as book-keeping" *Economics*, ibid., p.168.

[46] J M Keynes, 1923. *A Tract on Monetary Reform*. Macmillan, London.

[47] For those interested, a discussion of Keynes's *Tract* forms a key part of *Auditorial Central Banking*, New Economy Publications, Canterbury 2003.

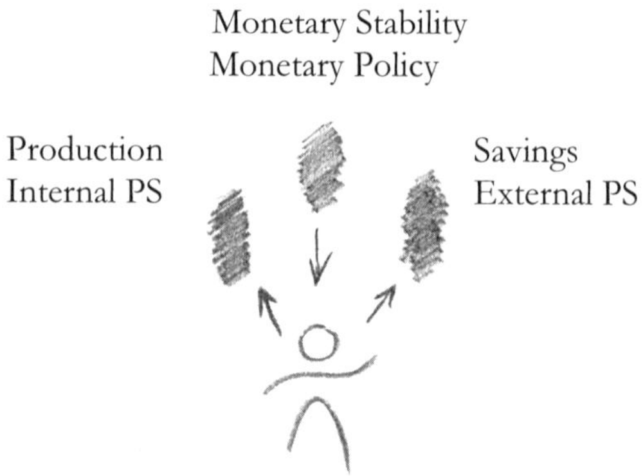

In seeking to go beyond the gold standard, Keynes wonders if the ways in which it operated could not be made into 'deliberate' and 'scientific' principles of policy. Like Steiner's, Keynes's argument also rests on the importance of recognising three main elements if economic life is to develop healthily – production, savings and the need for monetary stability ('integrity of money'). Production and savings he regards as the activity of free agents in the market place. Overseeing monetary stability, however, is a role for the 'controlling authority' (read central bank), acting on behalf of society at the behest of government – what one could call a societal, non-market role with a public good quality. In order that production and savings can develop healthily, monetary stability in turn relies on two main tasks – avoiding domestic inflation (internal price stability) and maintaining purchasing power parity with other currencies by way of *universally* floating exchange rates (external price stability).[48]

Keynes's *Tract* remains topical, despite the long years between the 1920s and 1980s, during which the state (in no small degree due to Keynes's influence) came to play a prominent part in monetary affairs, and despite the celebrated contrast between Keynes and Milton Friedman – loosely put, the economists of the left and right, statism and liberalism. The *Tract* still provides underpinning for the modern concept of central bank independence in which the central bank, being 'above the fray of self-seeking',[49] is responsible for the apoliti-

---

[48] I have added the word 'universally', but only, in my view, because Keynes's thesis requires it. Here is not the place to enter into the complex debate that would attend this point, however. Essentially, it means that *all* countries should float their exchange rates, not just some. The effect would be that all exchange rates became interdependent, reflections of one another, and not the result of the influence of any one country in particular.

[49] The image is from Capie, Goodhart and Schnadt: 'Central bankers are, perhaps, seen as having more in common with the judiciary, than with politicians or commercial bankers;

cal conduct of monetary policy in a context of floating exchange rates. Moreover, although 'Keynesian', it anticipates by a long way Milton Friedman's later 'own lights' dictum: '...flexible exchange rates are a means of combining interdependence among countries through trade with a maximum of internal monetary independence; they are a means of permitting each country to seek for monetary stability according to its own lights, without either imposing its mistakes on its neighbours or having their mistakes imposed on it. If all countries succeeded, the result would be a system of reasonably stable exchange rates; the substance of effective harmonisation would be attained without the risks of formal but ineffective harmonisation.'[50]

The point of illustrating these arguments with the three-element sketch is to make or at least suggest a conceptual link. Specifically

---

and are perceived as both technically expert, above the fray of self-seeking, and a necessary agent (of democratic government) for imposing order on a potentially unruly financial system.' *The Future of Central Banking*. Cambridge University Press, 1994, p.91.

50 Milton Friedman, 1966. *Essays in Positive Economics*. Chicago: Phoenix, p.200.

stated, Keynes was pointing to the institutional counterpart of Steiner's three kinds of money. For it has to be asked of Keynes: How would money be managed in a single global economy where so far the context has only been one of nations? And of Steiner: What is the institutional counterpart to three kinds of money and how does it relate to existing arrangements?

While Keynes thus points to the global financial architecture – with insights and practical suggestions that have lost none of their relevance – and thus to the macro level in the conventional sense, Steiner points in the micro direction to the nature of money in a single global economy – micro in the sense that it gives the individual consumer or firm the means to act globally.

If this argument holds water, it means that *all* economic activities, large and small and including those of government and central banks, could be accounted alike. If they were, they would then all act in accordance with the logic of accounting, even if their national (or fiat) currency denominations were retained.[51]

---

[51] This would also mean, very importantly, that monetary union did not require political union, which in world money

In this way, money as global bookkeeping would become the new gold standard.

This development has important consequences for the two questions asked of Keynes and Steiner. Could it be that they both point to the same answer, suggesting that associative economics may well be impliedly present? The more so if Keynes and Friedman do not in fact belong to different universes!

One twin development would bring the ideas of Steiner and Keynes (and even Friedman) together: the universalising of floating exchange rates already mentioned and the universal adoption of the central bank's right to set interest rates (operational independence). This would imply and require an end to governmental or political interference in monetary matters anywhere in the world. No longer able to set exchange rates – and therefore to influence capital flows as a means of competing against other countries – governments would thus cede central banks true independence by allowing them to set the

---

terms would mean global currency did not require global government. In fact, it requires governments to stay out of monetary matters and to confine their remit to the rights as between human beings and national *political* sovereignty.

inflation rate as well as the interest rate (goal as well as operational independence). This in turn would take the wind out of currency speculation, in the same but a freer way that currency union (fixed exchange rates) does at the moment.

But there is more… Such changes would require central banks to rest their understanding and involvement with money on the logic of accounting and away from fiat. But away, too, from the gold standard. In the process they would become societal rather than governmental agencies, listening or 'auditorial'[52] rather than instrumental in their overview role.

Of course, many forces and arguments are ranged against such a prospect, but they have one single origin. They derive from a refusal to enter the world such a landscape implies – a world in which national currency competition is given up and in which countries cooperate rather than vie for power, using the economy as a weapon. And a world, above all, in which human beings take direct responsibility for the

[52] 'Auditorial' is an invention, meant to convey the link between listening and auditing, but implying the active listening of an audience in an auditorium, rather than the inspecting nuance of an auditor.

'big' issues, especially the fact that the financial markets reflect myriad decisions of individual investors the world over.

All this revolves around the simple question discussed in chapter 13: Do we consider money as a thing in itself or as representative of economic processes we otherwise cannot see? The one means that money, not human beings, makes the world go round; the other makes the role of conscious human will paramount.

The 'big' issues are big because they require great force of will if we are to address, let alone remedy them; forces of will that cannot be engendered out of self-serving, but only when the individual acts in the name and on behalf of the global economy, humanity's common wealth.

Associative economics is thus all about enabling human beings to recognise, understand and give expression to this aspect of human nature. It is this that stands behind the idea of metamorphosing capitalism. The concept of power in economics (capital*ism*) is a matter of the human will directly. Metamorphosing capitalism, therefore, is about taking hold of one's will forces and putting them in service of the deeper purposes and potential of human history. It is not an easy matter, requiring us to understand, at least in outline terms, the complex issues touched on in this book. It is nevertheless a doable, and urgent, task.

The World in our Deeds

One last comment: It is a feature of modern economic life that day-to-day events are played out against a background of far-reaching debates about the nature of society, constitutional structures, and monetary matters. For the most part, however, even though their outcome determines the context of what they do, people feel these subjects remote – both conceptually and institutionally. To address this problem, we need to find ways to overcome this dichotomy by designing or envisaging a landscape, in which what we do on a so-called micro level is not different from the macro.

In associative economic terms, this means that every individual action, from a thought, to a decision, to an act of investment, should reflect hologrammatically, as it were, the single global economy in which it occurs and of which it is a part.

This contrasts greatly to the current image. In conventional economics, microeconomics refers to the decisions and behaviour of consumers and firms, and the efficient allocation of scarce resources by the optimising of such behaviour in determining price.[53] Macroeconomics studies the interactions of economy-wide variables – such as unemployment, inflation, and national income – independently of individual actors or their decisions.

The American economist, John Kenneth Galbraith, attributing this stark distinction to Keynes, describes it as 'one of the intellectually suffocating errors of modern economics'.[54] One can concur with Galbraith's view, since, whatever its author's intentions, a main effect of a construct that divides the economy in two in this way is to give rise to the idea that whatever individuals do and think is not really important. Indeed, macroeconomics

---

[53] Note, associative economics does not assume scarcity, or therefore Malthusian, let alone Darwinian, competition. It assumes that resources are or can be organised to be appropriate to human needs because it is within the gift and ability of human beings to organise economic life so that we are not victims to arbitrariness in such matters. Drought does not make for scarcity, for example, unless over the long run of harvests there has been no attempt to save for rainy days (to mix the metaphor), or if demagogic leaders starve their peoples or irresponsible corporations abuse their positions.

[54] J K Galbraith, 1987. *A History of Economics.* London, Hamish Hamilton, p.295.

deliberately aggregates and simplifies this element, encouraging the belief that the big picture has to be left to governments and experts, and behind them the wondrous workings of the invisible hand.

From an associative economic point of view, nothing could be further from the truth. The wider reaches of economic life derive from myriad individual actions, be they 'little', such as buying a train ticket, or 'big', as when setting the target inflation rate for a central bank. To divide the little from the big is a dangerous thing to do, and we should not be surprised if a world so conceived becomes characterised by policies that 'ordinary' people cannot own and do not care about, and a general belief that the individual is a powerless element. This is the opposite of current historical reality.

In associative economics, the terms micro and macro are also used but in a very different sense. Micro economic activity means individual actions – whether buying a stamp or investing in national infrastructure such as a railway system – that are microcosmic representations of global economic life as a whole. Macroeconomics is about the archetypal images underlying the precepts and policies for managing the economy. Since these precepts are given effect by individuals, the difference between micro and macro in associative economics does not entail a dichotomy between how we understand global economic reality (macro) and how we act within it (micro). Instead, one could say that the true nature of globalisation unfolds from practical decisions and arrangements that make the wide reaches of economic life their first consideration.

This, of course, has a huge implication for today's social, environmental, and even financial problems, most of which result from not including wider concerns in one's actions. When we send people back into the labour market, or throw litter on the ground, we think we are saving costs. In fact, we are merely pushing them onto our common balance sheet. The divorce between micro and macro in conventional economics indeed has much to answer for!

To behave associatively is the converse of all this. However small the action, it tells a different story and leads to a different landscape. The world to which this landscape belongs is not somewhere else – neither another planet nor another time. It exists as a potential all around us. If we would make it our social reality, we have but to step into it.

If this book can in any way help humanity take this step, it will have fulfilled its objective.

Associative Economics Institute Publications

A Human Response to Globalisation
Discovering Associative Economics
Marc Desaules
(Also in French)

The Metamorphosis of Capitalism
Realising Associative Economics
Christopher Houghton Budd

Step into Another World!
A Collaboration